Manai pирciceі ãapoд vин-

mamma.

1983. g. 28. окт..

The Egyptians

Text by
Jacques Champollion

MINERVA

The author of the text of this book is a grand-nephew of the eminent French scholar Jean-François Champollion, who first deciphered the hieroglyphs of ancient Egypt.

Credits : Archivio B/Ricciarini : 82 — British Museum : 80, 84a, b — Bulloz : 1, 6a, 10, 20, 21b, 42, 43, 45, 47, 50a, 75 — Carlo Bevilacqua : 73b — Cirani/Ricciarini : 13, 32 — Dulevant : 9 — Fiore : 89, 95 — Froissardey/Atlas : 22, 41 — Giraudon : 8c, 14, 44, 48, 49, 50b, 52a, 60, 65a, 66a, 67, 70, 71, 76, 78, 79, 81, 84c — Mathieu/Atlas : 21a — Metropolitan Museum, N.Y. : 57a, b, 61 — Pizzi/Chiari/Gemini : 24, 28, 34a, b, 35a, b, — S.E.F. : 5, 52c, 63c — Stierlin/Tourisme égyptien : 31a — Tenzi/Tourisme égytien : 16, 29, 31b, 37, 46, 72a, 83 — Tourisme égyptien : End papers, 2, 8b, 11, 15, 19, 25, 26, 27, 31a, b, 36a, b, 37, 39, 40, 58, 69, 73a, 77, 91, 94 — Unedi : 62, 64b, 66b, 68a, 72b — Viollet : 3, 8a, 31, 52b, d, 53, 55, 68c, 73c, 87a, b, 92a, b, 93, 96.

ISBN 0 - 517 - 351110

1 - The land of the Nile

Egypt: all was curious or mysterious in this ever distinguished land. The first pages in the annals of human history tell us of its great works and its glory. Its physical make-up was characterized by very special phenomena, and scientific progress has not at all weakened even today the powerful interest that these have always excited.

It seems that the ancient Greek philosophers had drawn from the Egyptian sanctuary the opinion which held that water was the basis of all things, that previously it was the structural material of the other parts of the globe, and that this principle of moisture, which was the mother and wet-nurse of beings, was called the Ocean by the Greeks and the Nile by the Egyptians. This was also the name of the great river which watered their country.

This river is in fact the eternal creator and conservator of the land of Egypt; it is to the rich silt, annually transported on its waters, that this country owes its existence; it is the

Typical landscape along the banks of the Nile. Above: offerings of flowers, grapes and dates.

Nile which forever maintains and renews fertility. Also, this munificent river was not only called as well the "most holy," the "father" and the "conservator of the country...," but was also considered a god, and was indeed the source of a religion with its own priests.

The Egyptians went so far as to regard their holy river as a tangible image of Ammon, their supreme deity; it was for them a palpable manifestation of this god who, in a visible form, vivified and preserved Egypt. The Greeks too, called the Nile the Egyptian Jupiter.

The Egyptian philosophers had also imagined the heavens to be divided as the earth; there was therefore a celestial Nile and a terrestrial Nile.

An author writes: "It is a sight worthy of wonder to see regularly each year, under a calm sky, without any signs of warning or visible cause, but as a supernatural power, the waters of a great river, wholly clear and limpid, suddenly change color at the very moment of the summer solstice, change beneath one's eyes into a river of blood, at the same time swelling, gradually rising to the autumn equinox and covering the surface of the surrounding country; then during an equally regularly determined period, diminish and withdraw little by little, returning to its

bed at the time other rivers are beginning to overflow."

But the effect of this phenomenon has had quite another importance for Egypt: the floodings of the Nile have created in the midst of the desert, the soil necessary for one of the most famous empires that ever existed; it has assisted nature in the very formation of this land, all of Lower Egypt being the result of the successive building up of land by the river.

One understands all the care the Egyptian government gave to the building of canals when one remembers that the fate of the country depended entirely upon the flooding of the Nile; if it failed completely, Egypt, so fertile, was struck barren, and famine destroyed the population. It was also recognized that if it were below normal, there was poverty; it was the same if the floods were over-abundant: these results depended entirely upon the quantity of rainfall in Abyssinia,

and no human means could regulate this according to the needs of the country. However, the wisdom of the Egyptian government surmounted these difficulties. It very soon understood that only the flooding of the Nile, reaching specific heights, could assure the abundance needed to guarantee the tranquillity of the people. The government undertook to prevent the harm which resulted from insufficient as well as excessive flooding, and to insure these tremendous results, had built a reservoir of water whose surface measures 150 square miles: this is the lake of Fayoum.

One presumes that the bed of Fayoum was previously a swamp. According to

Above: symbolic picture of a garden with a central pond (tomb of Rekhmire, 18th dynasty). Right: fowling scene.

4

ancient reports, the Pharaoh Moeris had a lake created on the area; if one admits that he had this lake dug in the western part of the province, considering that its perimeter was approximately 100 miles, and its depth considerable, it would follow that the Egyptians had to remove one trillion one billion (1,100,000,000,000) cubic meters of land, which can not be admitted; one must therefore admit that Moeris took advantage of the natural arrangement of the land to fix the lake here. A canal, drawn from the Nile and constructed across sands and rock, conducted the river's waters; toward the middle of the lake two pyramids rose to a great height, surmounted by a seated colossus, and because of this, Herodotus concluded that the lake had been dug by men's hands. But the pyramids could have been erected there before the low-lying area was covered by waters drawn from the Nile.

Moeris, who also bore the name Thutmosis in Greek history, reigned 1,700 years before Christ. His name is still carved in some of the greatest monuments of Thebes and Nubia; he received as well the titles of Patron of the Worlds and Servant of the Sun. The obelisk at Saint John Lateran in Rome had been erected in his honor in Egypt; there is also in the museum of Turin a statue of this king; it is of colossal proportions, in white-spotted black granite. Egyptian priests spoke of him to Herodotus, even though this prince was then already dead for more than one thousand years.

One can get an idea of Egypt's fertility by recalling that each month of the year the earth bears both flowers and fruits.

Among the vegetation observed in Egypt, some are indigenous while others are carried by the wind or the Nile. Among the trees peculiar to Upper Egypt one must count the palm, the doum and the sayal. The acacia nilotica is one of the trees that belongs to both Upper and Lower Egypt; others must be cultivated, such as the sycamore and the tamarind-tree, originating in the

Top left: fragment of papyrus (18th dynasty) in the Louvre. Bottom: detail of fresco, fruit trees depicted in a naive style.

interior of Africa, and the cordia myxa, the lebbeek acacia and the cassia fistula, coming from India. In Lower Egypt, which is easily flooded, grow the reeds, two kinds of white water lily or lotus, and finally the papyrus, formerly very common, today very rare in this country. There is some vegetation in the desert. In the watered lands clover and several other plants of the leguminous variety are sown.

Of all the plants in Egypt, the papyrus or byblos was one of the most useful in the prosperous times of this empire. It served as paper in the Orient, the Roman Empire and France even until the eleventh century. The papyrus grew in lakes and swamps, rising to about ten feet in height; its stem is surmounted by a tuft of hair which is unusable. To make writing papyrus with the stalk, one cut off the two ends, cut the stalk lengthwise into two equal parts, and separated, with a sharp instrument, the layers, about twenty in all, which form the stalk, whose diameter is two or three inches. The layers grow increasingly white as one nears the center. They were spread out separately, each one forming a sheet, and after several preparations, two sheets were glued together, one upon the other, in such a way that their fibers crossed; in this way the sheet was made sufficiently solid. One beat, pressed and polished each sheet, and with several glued together, made papers of varying lengths. One then coated the paper with cedar oil as a means of preserving it. Written on Eyptian papyrus we possess the charters of kings, emperors and popes, books in Greek and Latin dating from the earliest times of the French monarchy. But the antiquity of these written monuments is nearly negligible beside the Egyptian papyrus found in Egypt itself, in hermetically sealed argil jars, found in tombs. There are all kinds of papyrus found here: there are ritual or prayer-books for the dead, accounting documents, simple letters, trial records, and above all private contracts for sales or purchases, and other civil agreements. Some of these contracts written in Egyptian characters date even before Moses, and today are no less than 3,500 years old.

Above: the Nile in Upper Egypt; left and below: low-reliefs illustrating fishermen at work and the manufacture of a papyrus canoe. Right: ancient Egyptian boats.

2 - The laws of a society

A considerable number of social rules are cited by the writers of antiquity as the laws of ancient Egypt. An examination of these various rules would require, to arrive at a certain level of historic verity, a great deal of time and would present great difficulties. The ancient writers who spoke of these rules did not at all clearly distinguish the times of these laws, nor the different governments under which these laws, which did in fact exist, were carried out. To give a single example of this confusion of time, it will suffice to recall the law against counterfeiters, considered by Diodorus Siculus to number among the general laws of Egypt, along with and of equal importance to the oldest of these laws; and yet coined metals began in Egypt with the Persian rule. Common consent is that Darius' money or dariques was the first money legally introduced into Egypt by the Persian conquest. It seems that up to that time Egypt used only a conventional

sort of money for internal affairs, while for business outside the country gold or silver rings of a determined or verified weight were used. The distinction of the periods in the laws is therefore an essential factor in the study of this area of Egyptian institutions. Unable to undertake such a work here, we will restrict ourselves to recalling the main Egyptian laws whose memory has been preserved through time.

Perjury was punished by death; the oath being taken by the Egyptian legislation in many situations of great importance, one had to insure as much as possible the truth concerning God and man. It was the duty of all citizens to prevent crimes, to endeavor to carry out the punishment, and those who, seeing a man in danger, did not come to his aid, were considered as much criminals as the original offenders and were punished as such. Man had to defend his fellowman against an assailant, to guarantee him his greatest effort; if he could prove that he was incapable of this, then it was his duty to find the guilty party and carry the case to its just end. There was behind this law the idea that each crime and offence was a matter concerning the entire society, and that it was in the interest of each citizen that this crime or offence be punished;

Left: Prince Lahmes or Amosis (17th dynasty), as he can now be admired in the Louvre. Above: view of the impressive ruins of Luxor.

therefore, the right to pursue a crime was listed among man's duties, bestowed upon all citizens. The warrior had to atone for disobedience or the omission of a law of honor with a brilliant achievement. Crimes against women were punished with mutilation; the unfaithful woman was made ugly by the amputation of her nose; her adulterous partner was beaten. Those who told state secrets to the enemy had their tongue pulled out; one cut off the hand of the man who falsified weights, measures, the seals of princes or individuals, or of the writer who forged works or issued altered transcripts. One idea underlies these last laws, that of preventing the guilty party from committing the same crime twice. Physiologists today might well say that the Egyptians had also observed and recognized the influence of inner forces.

Egyptian society had known parricide, and it was punished by torture and the stake. Parents who killed one of their children were made to hold the dead body in their arms for three days and three nights; the law did not inflict death upon them for having taken life where they had given it. On the other hand, homicide was punished by death. Penal and criminal laws ware the same for both men and women; pregnant women, convicted of a capital crime, were judged and condemned only after they had given birth.

There are attributed to King Bocchoris, of the twenty-fourth dynasty, in the eighth century B.C., several laws relating to commerce. A debt was nullified if the debtor swore under solemn oath that he owed nothing to the creditor who did not have a written pledge. Unter no circumstances could the interest exceed the principal. The debtor's property was seized for his debts, but never the person himself. Herodotus attributes another law relating to commerce to another king of Bocchoris' century; this law enabled the Egyptians to make loans using their ancestor's mummies as pawn. The lender was then put in possession of the borrower's family tomb; it was only under such a condition that he could have the pawned mummies at his disposal, being forbidden however, to remove them from their site.

Under such circumstances, a debtor who did not pay his debt was deprived of the family burial rites and honors, and any children of his dying during this sacred pledge were treated likewise.

Among the other laws of ancient Egypt, we must cite the one which exempted sons from providing for their parents, and rather put the obligation on daughters. Circumcision was decreed, this law being merely a measure of public hygiene. Each individual was responsible for a yearly, written report, given to the magistrate of the region in which he was living, stating his name, his profession and the work which provided his livelihood; the same law punished by death anyone not making such a declaration or anyone unable to indicate his legal means of existence. Diodorus Siculus says in fact that those who wished to follow the profession of thief had to register with the man at the head of this class, and bring him all the fruits of his industry. Those who had had their goods stolen also made a written declaration to the same thief-chief describing the objects which had been stolen from him, as well as the time and place they had been taken. With this information the said objects were identified and evaluated, the owner then abandoning one quarter of the goods to the society of thieves. Many comments have been made on this ununsual system; and admitting its reality, perhaps we only need look upon such an arrangement of the social order with human passions, as is seen in contemporary socities.

Diodorus Siculus mentions several other Egyptian laws, but always without indicating the times in which they were enforced, and without bothering to distinguish the influences exerted on Egyptian legislation by the invasion and customs of the Persians and Greeks when they were the masters of Egypt. It was, for example, under the Greeks that a marriage between a brother and sister was allowed; the history of the Kings of Ptolemy offers frequent examples; we can find none from earlier periods. During this same period it also seems that the annulling of a marriage was very easily authorized by the laws.

It would, however, be reckless to state that polygamy was authorized. It is agreed

that this was expressly prohibited in the priesthood; it would be most difficult to prove that this was not the case as well for all other classes. Monogamy seems to have been the general situation of Egyptian families. If there was evidence contrary to this in the written laws, princes, and priests, the most influential people of the State, must have, by their all-powerful example passed on to the empire, changed the law by their own habits. As for women, nothing leads us to believe that they were in an inferior civil position to men, thereby giving additional support to the argument for monogamy.

History has noted several essential modifications introduced into Egyptian legislation, among others the repeal of the death penalty by Sabbacon, the head of the Ethiopian dynasty who by conquest established himself in Egypt about 700 B.C. This king substituted for that punishment the sentence of penal servitude for life.

Columns of the temple of Hathor (goddess of love and joy) at Denderah, north of Luxor.

3 - The Pharaohs

Royal tombs exist in considerably great number in Egypt: the tombs of the kings of the eighteenth, nineteenth and twentieth dynasties, originating from Thebes, can still be seen in the valley of Biban-el-Molouk, which is an annex of the ancient capital. Here follow excerpts from the description of the tombs, such as Champollion saw them:

"The valley of Biban-el-Molouk, formerly Biban-el-Ourou, hypogeum of kings, was the royal necropolis, a perfect location chosen for this purpose, an arid valley, enclosed by high, steep cliffs or crumbling mountains, almost all with great clefts, producing either extreme heat or rocky landslides,

"Entering the valley from the most remote point, a narrow opening clearly man-made, and still offering a few remaining pieces of Egyptian sculpture, one soon sees at the foot of the mountains, or on the slopes, square doors, for the most part cumbrous, so that one must approach them more closely

Tutenkhamen in the form of the god Harakty. Above and following pages: the temple of Queen Hatshepsut—an astonishing sight in the midst of the imposing landscape of Deir el-Bahari. Hatshepsut was the first woman to mount the Egyptian throne.

in order to see their decoration: these doors, which are all quite similar, are the entrances to the king's tombs. Each tomb has its own door, since formerly there was no communication whatsoever among them,

"It took me some time, after arriving at Biban-el-Molouk, to assure myself that the tombs were indeed, as I had previously deduced after considerable deliberation, those of the kings belonging to all the Theban dynasties, that is to say, to the princes whose family was originally from Thebes. A quick examination of the excavations before ascending to the second cataract, and the stay of several months upon my return, these fully convinced me that these hypogeums contained the bodies of the kings of the eighteenth, nineteenth and twentieth dynasties, the three of which are in fact Diospolitan or Theban dynasties.

"... The great chamber in the tomb of Ramses V, the one containing the sarcophagus, surpasses the others in dimension and magnificence. The ceiling, a great carved vault with a splendid curve, had retained all its painting. The freshness of the painting is such that one must be accustomed to the miracles of conservation in Egyptian monuments in order to convince oneself that fragile colors have held up through thirty centuries. The walls of this vast chamber,

from base to ceiling, are covered with sculpted and painted scenes as are found in the rest of the tomb, and are covered with hieroglyphs in explanatory inscriptions; the sun is still the principal subject of these bas-reliefs, of which a great number contain, in emblematical form, the entire cosmogonic system and the general principles of physics as known by the Egyptians.

The laws of the State reserved certain special rites for the sons of kings: they were dressed in a particular costume; the pedum, and a fan made from a long ostrich feather set in an elegant handle were their characteristic symbols.

The prince, so designated by the order of primogeniture, succeeded to the paternal throne; religion sanctified his succession, the gods themselves putting the royal institution in his hands.

The queen was near the king during the coronation; she was beside the monarch in other public ceremonies as well. Other domestic scenes provide additional proof of the honorable position of women in Egypt, as constant companions to men, sharing domestic authority with them.

One of the first royal duties, and the one which when accomplished was the most pleasure for men and gods, was the construction of religious edifices, adorned with colossuses and obelisks. It was at Luxor that Sesostris dedicated his magnificent building to Ammon.

The queen and the sons and daughters of the king took part in all these ceremonies, and their rank and places were assigned. To the crowd of gods that the king had to honor, he religiously added his own ancestors; his father and mother received the first respects, then his ancestors, sometimes in great number, arranged by descending generations; the king burned incense, according to existing records, in honor of his father's fathers and his mother's mothers. This custom, which was connected to the profoundly moral and innate idea in the spirit of the Egyptian nation, the respect of the elderly and the worship of ancestors, was not done away with by the foreign conquerors of Egypt.

When a war was undertaken, the protection of the gods was invoked in public ceremonies, and the king took command of the army. The army went on campaign; different armed troops took their place in the marching line, eight or ten abreast. A trumpet and a group of hoplites, heavily armed infantry, preceeded a chariot from which there rose a mast, topped by a ram's head decorated with the disk of the sun: it was the symbol of the god Ammon-Ra guiding the army against the enemy. The king, mounted on his war chariot, followed behind the god; he was escorted by bowmen of the guard, and followed by his own officiers. As soon as the enemy was reached, the battle was taken up; divine protection gave victory to the king of Egypt who, immediately afterwards, addressed the heads of his troops who presented him with the enemy's token prisoners, with each company giving a written account of the number of right hands and other limbs cut from the dead enemy on the battefield. Egyptian soldiers were armed with helmets, long-bows, quivers, battle axes and lances. One part of the army, in battle order and made up of heavily armed foot-soldiers or hoplites, marched in front; light troops were in the flanks; war chariots formed the back line. The king was in the center.

The army marched in divisions: the king on his chariot, whip in hand, led his horses, richly caparisoned; groups of chained prisoners followed him; officers held large parasols above him. He entered the royal city of Thebes on foot; rows of prisoners, held among the various conquered hords, followed him; first he was to go to the temple to give thanks to the gods for his victory and honor them with his captives.

The palace was made up of several main buildings, courtyards and pavilions, large and small suites of apartments. The main façades were broken by beautiful windows, decorated in fine taste; the building, made entirely of stone, was three stories high.

One of the outstandingly beautiful giant statues of Luxor.

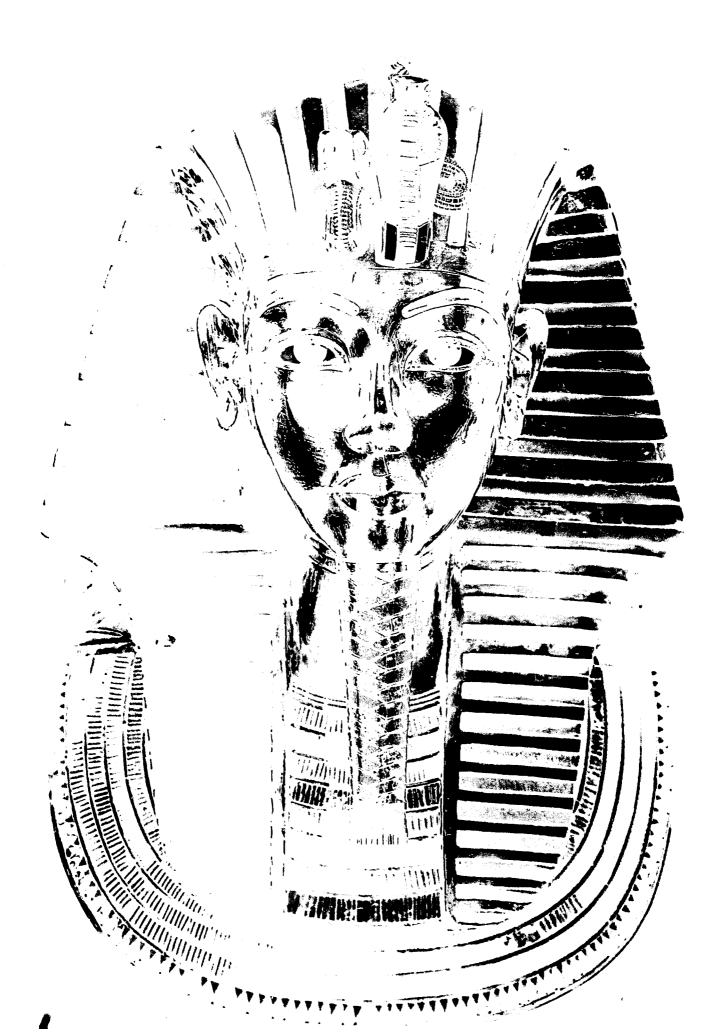

It was a true family dwelling; the king lived there at ease with his wife and children; they played in his presence, even with him, and her royal majesty bowed to such paternal tenderness. The king dined with his family or alone; he was served by women of the palace. Always intermingled with the luxurious and elegant furniture, with the sumptuous surroundings, were the most graceful natural elements: vases of flowers decorated the salons, garlands of greenery were combined with the rich decorations. When the king left the palace, if he did not mount his chariot, he was carried on a palanquin, or in a carriage which was a beautifully decorated chamber with two folding doors, placed on a sleigh. Included in the royal household were dogs, cats and monkeys, and from even before 1,500 B.C., dwarfs, who were meant to entertain Egyptian lords and their society, just as in 1,500 A.D., dwarfs belonged to the feudal barons of Europe. Companies of musicians, male and female dancers were also admitted to the king's palace in order to vary amusements.

Our various ideas on the State and royal families have been gotten from the remaining monuments of Egypt.

After the gods, it was the kings upon whom the public voice bestowed its honors; and after the cities' vying with each other in their bas-reliefs, in which the courage and godliness of the kings was celebrated, there was no more flattering work of art than the colossal portraits, erected in the courtyards

The celebrated treasure of Tutankhamun: his funeral mask and two of his sarcophagi (Cairo Museum).

of the great temples. The Memnonium of Thebes gives us proof and an example.

"It is toward the far end of these ruins," wrote Champollion, "and beside the still rising river, dominating the plain of Thebes, that we find the two famous colossi, about sixty feet high, of which the northern one is so celebrated, under the name of the Colossus of Memnon. They are each carved from a single block sandstone, transported from the quarries of upper Thebaid, and placed on immense bases of the same rock, both representing seated Pharaohs, their hands placed on their knees, in peaceful poses.

"According to all indications, these two colossi decorated the exterior façade of Amenophion's main pylon; and despite the

state of ruin to which they have been reduced by barbarity and fanaticism, one can still imagine the elegance, the great care and research that had gone into their execution, judging by the accessory figures which

At the desert's edge and facing the rising sun: the Colossi of Memnon (fifty feet high without their bases), carved from pink sandstone.

decorate the back part of the throne of each colossus. They are standing figures of women, sculpted from the same mass as each monolith, of no less than fifteen feet in height. The magnificence of their coiffure and the rich detail of their dress are in perfect harmony with the rank of men whose memory they recall for us."

4 - The obelisk

It is not possible to say at what time the first obelisk was erected; historic tradition attributes this kind of monument to the most ancient kings; but no obelisk dates before the eighteenth Egyptian dynasty, which was in the year 1822 B.C. There exist several obelisks of the princes of the eighteenth dynasty and their successors. The great majority of Egyptian kings had them erected. Cambyses' violence destroyed a great number of obelisks in the main cities, particularly in Thebes. It is also said that struck by the magnificence and the majesty of one of the obelisk raised by the king Ramses in this large city, the mad conqueror had a fire stopped which was threatening to destroy this monument. Historians say that the king who had it erected, in order to guarantee the protection of this precious work, and to assure the proper care by the architect and workers who were erecting it, had his son attached to the top of the obelisk.

Left and above: at Karnak, the ruins of the main temple and the obelisk of Queen Hatshepsut.

When Egypt was reduced to the rank of a Roman province, Augustus understood to what extent his monumental spoils could brilliantly enhance the eternal city, and so had two obelisks from Heliopolis transported to Rome. Caïus Caligula demanded a third one, and according to Pliny's report, the sea had never seen a ship of such colossal proportions as the one which was built for this purpose. Other emperors imitated Augustus' example; eleven obelisks and the remains of several others still exist in Rome;

The English word *obelisk*, which has been commonly replaced by the word *needle*, is Latin for *obeliscus*, diminutive of the Greek *obelos*, meaning pointed pillar. The word obelisk therefore means a small pointed pillar, attributed to the Alexandrian Greeks, men of caustic, clever spirit, having given this name to these giant blocks of granite, more than one hundred feet long.

Obelisks are essentially historic monuments, placed in front of temples and palaces, telling in their inscriptions the incentive for the building of these edifices, their purpose and their dedication to one or more of the country's deities; inscriptions on obelisks give construction details and the name and relations of the princes who erected them; they indicate the development or adornments made by these princes' efforts, and thusly the relative period of each part of the edifice. Lastly, obelisks themselves are mentioned in inscriptions as one of the religious acts of the Pharaohs.

The Egyptians never thought of putting a single obelisk in the center of a vast space where it would have simply disappeared. Two obelisks were raised in front of the pylon or main entrance of a temple; they majestically announced the edifice and were as well one of the first signs of glory of the prince who had had them built in honor of the gods of the country.

The village of Luxor is part of the territory of Thebes, on the right bank of the Nile. A region of ruins attracts the traveler here, and it is toward the north end of this area that we find the picturesque entrance to the palace. It is a pylon, composed of two pyramidal blocks between which there is a door; that of the palace of Luxor is no less than fifty-two feet high, and is topped with

an elegant cornice; the pylons are eighteen feet higher, running ninety-two feet from each side of this door.

The subjects sculpted in bas-relief on the pylon are of great historical interest. The immense surface of each of the two massive blocks is covered with finely styled sculpture depicting several hundred figures in military scenes. There is the king Ramses the Great (Sesostris), seated on his throne in the middle of his camp, receiving his military chiefs and foreign delegates; we also see the details of the camp, the baggage, tents, wagons, etc.

These two scenes are each about fifty feet long; they are preceded by the two obelisks which are first to strike the traveler's eye and spirit.

A quarry of the finest quality pink granite, situated at Syen, toward Egypt's southern border at the first cataract, supplied the stone for these two obelisks. They are both made of single blocks, or monoliths. Their surfaces have achieved a brillant polish; their angles are sharp and well drawn, but the obelisks surfaces are not exactly flat. There is a slight convexity, and they are so precisely executed that one is astounded by the science of the architect.

The four sides of the obelisks are covered with hieroglyphic inscriptions. A quick inspection suffices to indicate that on each side the signs are symmetrically arranged to form three perpendicular columns, quite distinct, forming three inscriptions on each side.

The total number of signs on the obelisk is upwards of 1,600; they are as much faithful portraits as they are representative objects, and we can understand that this fidelity, this complete science of an iconography which could include all the objects of the material world, expressed in these Egyptian inscriptions a fundamentally basic nature, since each sign had its own clearly precise meaning.

Left and right: assorted obelisks now at Luxor and Cairo.

5 - Priests, practices and sciences

The priesthood was, properly speaking, the educated and informed group of the nation. It was especially dedicated to the study of the sciences and the progress of the arts; in addition it was responsible for religious ceremonies, the administration of justice, and the raising of taxes.

Original account-books from the temples have come down to us, and we can quite assuredly affirm that these receipts include products other than just revenues from the priesthood; various payments in kind were made at the temples in Egypt; the citizens' piety was not fruitless, and where monies in metal were not to be had, the products of the earth or industry were undoubtedly the normal means of exchange; precious metals were only one kind of exchangeable value.

In addition to the numerous revenues made at the temples to the living, we must mention those made to the dead; it has been esta-

blished that in Thebaid, mummies that did not have private tombs were buried in a common tomb belonging to a city, or a section of a city if it was that large; on these mummies' coffins, more or less richly styled, there was written, as we can see on all the known tombs, the name and relations of the deceased. In earlier times one even attached a small wooden tablet on which the name and relations were also written. Identified in this way, the coffins were then placed in immense tombs carved into the mountains, and where we can still see evidence of these mummies piled up by the thousand; the property and protection of these tombs were in the hands of the priests, and all mummies residing here were obliged to pay a fixed tax each year which continually increased. There are existing contracts which bear witness to this fact, and which tell us as well that the priests sold the rights to collect taxes on the tombs for a certain number of years to farmer-generals of revenues who, with others of their kind subcontracted for one or more tombs in particular; and in this contract we find a roll of the names of the mummies who, in each tomb, annually payed this lodging tax. It is in this way that the living and the dead united to make rich the temples and maintain the power of the priesthood, by dint of the law and the piety of kings

The remains of one of the temples of Abydos. This site, which is quite difficult to reach, is one of the most remarkable in Egypt.

and citizens.

It is worthy of note however, that the royal treasury also collected several taxes on the temples, perhaps as a means of moderating, with public consent, the accumulated wealth of a class ever powerful by its moral influence.

Two other obligations, imposed on the priesthood at the crown's profit, seemed a bit strange, and will indicate with certainty the degree of superiority to which the military class, from which the royal family had come, had achieved over the priestly class, formerly holding such power in all other matters of state. Each priest payed a duty to the king for his initiation into the mysteries.

The other unusual custom was that all those belonging to the priestly class were obliged to make a voyage by water to Alexandria each year.

Thusly, in territorial possession, the entire priesthood was like a family with a vast inheritance, transmissible, according to known conditions, to its various members from generation to generation. These hereditary rights to land bore with them the hereditary obligation of priestly duties, because the nature of these duties determined the cohereditary share reverting to each member of the family: it is on this basic principle that the entire Egyptian priesthood was founded.

Thusly, the priests married and their sons were priests. The great number of places of devotion, their rich endowments and the fertility of Egypt, these all easily explained how such a great number of priests could live in such affluence; and to these endowments and callings one must add the grants received from the royal treasury for the numerous salaried duties which were reserved for their cast, including all the branches of public administration which were not specifically military. Therefore priests' families were made secure for life by the possible transmission of a share of the general inheritance, proportioned to the number of family members; they were also guaranteed their rank in the hierarchy of the priesthood, as this was also hereditary.

The high priest, supreme ruler of the order, was the first state official after the king.

Herodotus was shown the chronological series of statues of the high priests; they were in the temple, beside the group of royal statues. The sons of the highest officers of the church lived with the monarch's sons.

The priests also practiced medicine et surgery; each physician had to devote himself to one kind of illness; this was a means of better acquainting himself with the problem, and if possible, of solving it.

The Egyptians' talent for observation and their special aptitude in natural research remains incontested: no nation has better know itself than the school of learned priests knew Egypt, and no public administration gave better counsel and advice in the public interest, than that which grew out of this knowledge. It is certain that the annual uniformity of the principal physical phenomena both simplified the study and further assured the results of advice. This immense and marvelous flooding of the Nile, coming each year on the same day, leaving Egypt under its waters for the same length of time, untilled and barren, its wandering population on a sea for several months; then the waters' retreat, giving the land a new surface and the human race which lived upon it an activity which was stopped by nothing until the inevitable return of the same phenomenon; this regularity, this providential predestination, infallibly imprinted order and foresight on the nation's character.

Of all the precepts, of all the protective efforts, the precious results of this attentive solitude which characterized Egypt's public administration in its times of splendor, there is one of which we must make particular mention because of its unequaled importance. We wish to speak of mummies, of the mummification of dead bodies, an institution both political and religious, and as well a measure of public hygiene, sanctioned by the divine authority, sanctified by religious concurrence.

After the retreat of the Nile's waters, the land is covered with the silt they have deposit-

Top: the goddess Hathor, as depicted on the columns of the temple of Isis at Philae; below: the entrance to the temple of Nefertari at Abu-Simbel.

ed and the remains of all kinds of animals that have been submerged in the flood. After the Nile's retreat, the rising temperature quickly dries the silt, and the animal remains, after a long period under water, promptly putrefy; the atmosphere is polluted with this decaying, and plague strikes and cuts down the unexpecting population. Ancient Egypt, with its everflooding Nile, stopped the source of this deadly pestilence, preventing the decay of animal matters by enbalming them in the various abundant elements of the country; and the clever combination of this prophylactic measure with ideas of nation and family created the respect and worship of ancestors, one of the most beneficial and moral beliefs in the wisdom of Egypt. The land was freed from the plague's scourge. All antiquity bears witness to the endless healthful well-being of Egypt, and no tales of epidemics destroying the old world cite Egypt as suffering from their cruel effects. Delivered by mummification from decaying animals, there remained Egypt's climate, without rain or clouds, the most healthy products, and the world's purest water.

The history of plagues and epidemics observed from the sixteenth to the eighteenth century A.D. is most unanimous on one point: all plagues, the true plagues that afflicted the East and West, came from Egypt; Egypt is the birth-place of plagues; each year it was cruelly struck; however, the plague was unknown in ancient Egypt during its many centuries. What occurred in Egypt during this long interval for such a healthful reign be followed by such deadly scourge, starting with the sixteenth century A.D.? It is that from this century on, the custom and obligation of mummifying the dead stopped: the Fathers of the desert who preached Christianity on the banks of the Nile, and Saint Anthony above all, who died in 356, strongly forbade the new Christians, under threat of eternal damnation, from imitating the pagans, their ancestors, who enbalmed the bodies of their relations, surrounding them as well with devilish symbols and ornaments; one listened and then followed these pious and ignorant preachings repeated over a century; one no longer created mummies, and 543 is the year of the first bubonic plague Egypt gave to the world; it ravaged Europe for half a century, and every year, after the flood's retreatring waters, Egypt felt its more or less deadly effects, more or less contagious for its neighboring nations.

It is also in the sanctuaries that precise sciences were studied and perfected, and where research was carried out for applications of general usefulness. Astronomers were also priests; and the vast platforms of the temples served as observatories.

The results of their observations taught them that the appearance of certain stars, after a period of several centuries, no longer corresponded to the same seasons, and that they had taken note of this movement

Detail from a low-relief on the pylon at the entrance to the Temple of Luxor.

and change. They divided the heavens into constellations; their names and forms were closely related to Egypt's concepts and attitudes. The invention of the zodiac was their work, dating back to earlier than 2,500 B.C. The civil calendar was regulated according to the established Sothic cycle. The year was composed of 365 days, divided into 12 months of 30 days each, followed by five complementary days. There was also the week, or period of seven days, one of the oldest vestiges of civilization. It is believed the number of days in the week was

At Karnak, the Courtyard of Ramses II and the pink granite statue of the pharaoh and his wife, Nefertari.

Top right: columns of the funerary temple of Queen Hatshepsut at Deir el-Bahari. Bottom: the famous Avenue of the Sphinxes outside the Temple of Amon, at Karnak.

Above: an almost unreal view of the temple of Philae, during the Nile flood. Below: the courtyard of the Temple of Luxor and the great rock temple of Ramses II at Abu-Simbel.

drawn from the number of planets then known, and that the names of the days were given those of these heavenly bodies.

Thusly we will learn that in our time as in antiquity, the first day of the week was that of the moon, the second was that of Mars, the third of Mercury, the fourth of Jupiter, the fifth of Venus, the sixth of Saturn, and the seventh of the sun, or the day of God;

In this way, Egypt has come down to us today, regulating with religious authority one of our main public institutions, the most common division of time, the one which has prevailed over other systems proposed by science, or the authority of church or state.

Diodorus Siculus reports the following: "The priests coach the children in their studies of arithmetic and geometry; this is because each year the flooding of the Nile destroys property boundaries, disputes arise among neighbors, and geometry is the only means of solving them. Arithmetic also serves for social purposes, and geometric speculations. It is especially useful for those who follow astrology, since the Egyptians, like other peoples, observe the movements of the stars, and keep records which date back for an incredible number of years, their having studied this from the earliest times. They have carefully described movements, the courses and positions of planets, and the good or bad influence of each of these on peoples' births, often concluding from these certain predictions in men's lives."

Porphyry knew that Egyptians priests spent part of the night in purifications, the other part observing stars. Strabon saw at Heliopolis an immense edifice that was the home of priests devoted especially to the study of philosophy and astronomy; and Diodorus adds to this by saying that Egyptian priests predicted the future as much through the science of things as through the stars. Clement of Alexandria, who had seen the end of pharaonic institutions in Egypt, places in the order of the priesthood, the priest responsible for the horoscope before the holy scribe. He held in his hands, said the holy Father, a clock, and a phoenix, symbol of astrology, Thoth's four books of

astrology always held in its beak; the first of these books dealt with wandering and stable stars; the second with the connections and illumination of the sun and the moon; the last two with the rising of these two bodies. Lastly, according to a report by Choeremon in Porphyry, the horoscope priest was well above the crowd of other priests.

All ancient traditions name Chaldea and Egypt as the birthplaces of astrology, and we note in passing that this clearly established fact is new evidence that communications existed between these two countries. As for Egypt, very early given to the practice of astrology, Cicero formally tells us that the Egyptians are considered well acquainted, for a great number of centuries, with the Chaldean science which, based on the daily observation of the stars, predicts the future and man's destiny. Before Cicero, Herodotus had said, "The Egyptians are the authors of several inventions, such as determining, according to the day a man is born, which events he will encounter in life, how he will die, and what his character and spirit will be." It is to two Egyptians, made famous in Greek and Roman antiquity by this report, named Petosiris and Necepso, that the basic works of Egyptian astrology are attributed. But the period in which these two scholars lived and wrote is highly doubtful: on one hand, they are placed in Sesostris' century; on another Necepso is confused with the king of Egypt in the 26th dynasty, who bore the same name; but it is certain that Ptolemy and Proclus looked upon these two astrologers as very ancient, and that neither Pliny nor any other Greek or Latin author doubted the authenticity of their works; new evidence of Egyptian origin are writings bearing their names and the doctrine they embraced, in which the theme of the world's birth and the theory of decans dominate.

Priests' costumes varied, being as strictly regulated as their hierarchy, with general

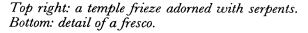

Top right: a temple frieze adorned with serpents. Bottom: detail of a fresco.

obligations imposed upon all members of the cast; in addition there were the customs and injunctions belonging to each order of priest.

As the first general rule of Egyptian priests, we must mention as of prime importance their need to be completely shaven and depilitated; it was an imperial duty for them to perform this every three days. In this command was the idea of absolute bodily purity and cleanliness, demanded in the priests' dealings with the gods and the administration of holy duties. In Egyptian monuments from all periods, we can easily recognize a priest of any order by his shaven and depilitated head.

Circumcision was prescribed for all Egyptians, priests as well as citizens.

Following Egypt's example, the Jewish

priesthood prescribed these same laws to its members; a dead insect on the skin or in the clothing of a Jewish priest rendered him liable to severe punishment. Ceanliness and the choice of fabrics for the garments of certain groups or individuals, was, at all times among nations on all levels of development, a most clear sign of superiority. This simple means of influence was not lacking among the Egyptian masses; its priests, also free of any bodily deformity, could only be dressed in linen cloth; the use of woolen fabrics was forbidden. One has searched for the hidden motives for such a law, using the most occult secrets of the material and religious in trying to find possible answers; it was said that wool, hair and horse-hair came from impure sources; linen is born from the immortal earth. The truth is that linen made up into very fine, light garments of a brilliant whiteness, appropriate for all seasons, and containing no impure taint. These garments had to be outstanding; those who wore them were immediately distinguished in a crowd whose fabrics were common and coarse. In summary,

the law concerning priests' clothing ordered that they be dressed more cleanly and richly than the rest of the Egyptian population. The ancients say that this brilliantly white costume, the habitually severe expressions and the walk and manner of speaking of the priests, resulted in a most imposing exterior, completed by the strained attitude of arms and hands constantly hidden in the folds of the garments; monuments confirm these observations.

In all religious ceremonies, priests used various utensils and instruments made from different materials, and our museums contain almost all of those seen in monuments. The perfumes offered to the gods were burned in an *amschir* or a bronze incenser in the shape of a cup placed in a hand coming out of a lotus stem. Small chests in the same material, inlaid with ivory or various colored woods, contained perfumes.

Luxor: views of the temple, its façade and the obelisk (the twin of which was taken by Bonaparte to Paris, where it now adorns the Place de la Concorde).

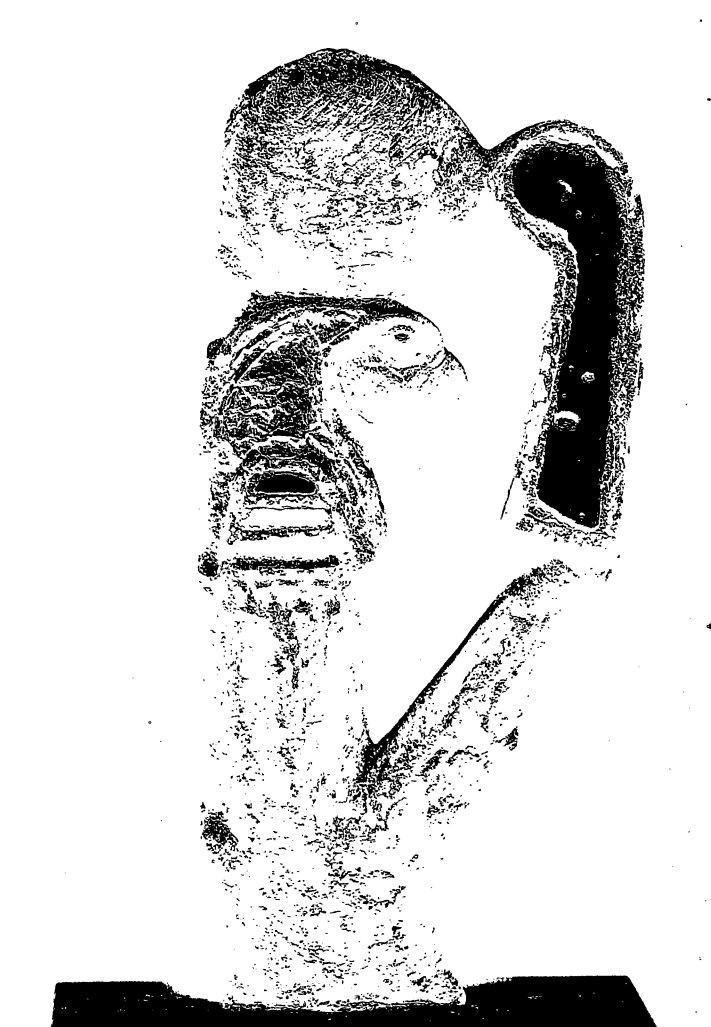

6 - Beliefs

According to the sacred history of Egypt, it was Thoth, the original Hermes, the Trismegistus, or three times greater, who wrote all the books by the supreme order of God. This first Thoth was the celestial Hermes, or divine intelligence personified, the only one of the divine beings who, from the beginning of things, could understand the essence of this supreme God. He had, according to the sacred myths of Egypt, recorded this great knowledge in the books which remained unknown until the demiurge created souls, and consequently the material universe at the same time as the human race. The first Hermes had written these books in divine or sacred language and scriptures; but after the cataclysm, when the physical world was reorganized and given a new existence, the Creator, taking pity on men who lived without rules and laws, wanted, in giving them intelligence and the correct control, that they follow the path which would lead them to His bosom, from

which they had gone astray. It was then that Isis and Osiris appeared, their special duty being the civilizing of the human species. This couple had as an associate and faithful adviser, Thoth, also called Thoyth by the Greeks, who was the second Hermes, and the incarnation of the first, or celestial Hermes, manifest on earth.

All that Isis and Osiris tried to take man out of his savage state was either suggested or approved by Thoth, and it is to this second Hermes that the Egyptians thought themselves indebted for all their social institutions. Men were still reduced, like animals, to manifesting their feelings through confused and uncoordinated outcries; Thoth taught them an articulate language, and by giving a name to all objects, gave each individual the means of making known his ideas and learning those of others. In addition, he taught them to set them down in a lasting manner, by inventing art and writing; he organized the social state; he established religion and regulated its ceremonies; he introduced to men astronomy and the science of numbers, geometry and the use of weights and measures. Not satisfied by fulfilling merely the needs of human society with his important and useful creations, the second Hermes also set about contributing all he could to embellish life: he invented music,

Left: the god Ra (Louvre). Above: fragment of the Bull Tablet (schist; Abydos, pre-Thinite period).

43

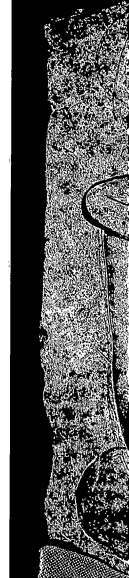

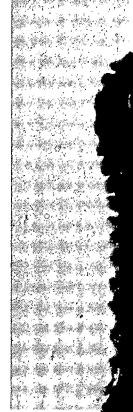

created the lyre, to which he gave only three strings, and instituted gymnastic exercises. And lastly, it is this god who made known to man architecture, sculpture, painting, and all the useful arts. This is what Plato, Plutarch, and many other authors have told.

For the Egyptians, Thoth was the author of all known books; a great number were attributed to him. There were in fact, in Egypt, considerable libraries and archives. In the magnificent edifice called the tomb of Osymandyas by Greek antiquity, there was a library of sacred books, and on its door was written "remedy of the soul".

Books existed in such great quantity in Egypt that the number of works attributed to Hermes was, according to Iamblic, twenty thousand, and an even greater number in Manethon's estimation; Hermes is also the scholarly cast and science itself in Egyptian thought. Sacred books were the most studied, and one considered as such those which dealt with nature, and the hierarchy and worship of the gods; a king named Suphis, to whom the great pyramid is attributed, was the author of one of these treatises. One also considered as sacred, historic books comprising the nation's annals, the great works of kings and illustrious citizens; these books were deposited in the temples' archives.

No work of ancient literature is better known than the writings gathered under the common heading of the Hermetic Books; they are written for the most part in Greek, by whom and when no one knows. Those who wrote them in this language state that they translated them from texts of sacred Egyptian scriptures. A close examination brings to light ideas which are foreign to the Egyptian world, born of varying sects in

times subsequent to those of Pharaonic splendors, and were therefore interpolated into the ancient text, as it to give them some merit by means of this alleged source. Champollion studied them thoroughly, and stated publicly, despite certain rash or bold criticisms of the times, that these books did indeed contain a bulk of purely Egyptian traditions, always in agreement with the most authentic monuments of Egypt.

Among the fragments that have come down to us, one notices that of a discourse of Hermes, directed to Thoth: "It is difficult for the mind," he said, "to conceive of God, and for the tongue to speak of Him. One can only describe an incorporeal thing with material means; and that which is eternal can be incorporated with that which is subject to time only with the greatest of difficulty. One expires, the other exists forever. One is a reality... that which can be known by the eyes and the senses, like visible bodies; that which is incorporeal, invisible, spiritual, without shape, cannot be known by our senses: I understand, therefore O Thoth, I understand that God is ineffable!"

"Death," he adds, "is a pain which strikes some men with a profound terror. This is ignorance. Death arrives through the weakness and dissolution of the parts of the body; the body dies because it can no longer carry its being; what one calls death is merely the destruction of the body and the senses (the being, the soul, does not die)."

"The truth," he further adds, "is that which is eternal and immutable; truth is the first of all goods; the truth does not and cannot exist on earth; it is possible that God gave some men, along with the faculty of thinking of divine things, that which enables them to think of truth as well; but nothing is truth on earth, because all things there are material, a bodily form subject to change, alteration, corruption, new combinations. Man is not truth, because all that is true is that which derived its essence from itself, and remains that which it is."

Three renderings of Egyptian woman: holding a papyrus on her knees, eating a duck (whole!) and in profile, with a typical hairdo.

7 - Family, daily life

All historians of antiquity place the military class or cast in the second rank of the social organization of Egypt,

The existence of this powerful cast dates back to the beginnings of Egypt's civil foundations; under the theocracy, it was also the second rank of the State; it became the first when soldiers, tired of obeying a priest-king, chose the most illustrious among its ranks, raised their shields and exercising supreme authority, had men take the place of gods, thus founding the dynasties of kings, recognizing Menes as the leader of the new system of government.

Herodotus mentions an army of four hundred and ten thousand men, a number perhaps applying only to the historian's own period. At this time, Egypt had suffered painful invasions, namely those of the Ethiopians and Persians; Egyptian prosperity had considerably declined, and its decadence was approaching. In its days of splendor, under the kings of the eighteenth dynasty, the military population proportionate to that

Left: a Hathoric column. Hathor was known as the 'goddess with the cow's ears' and protected Queen Hatshepsut. Above: knife handle from Djebel Arak (Louvre).

of all of Egypt, must have been considerably greater.

Egypt, for a long period surrounded by uncultivated and barbarous nations, must have had, for security reasons, strong military provisions on all its borders. The majority of its wars were defensive. Nomadic tribes and neighboring countires, attracted by its riches and fertility, constantly threatened Egypt; and several times Egypt was powerless to the opposition. The Ethiopian border was guarded by its united forces at Elephantine, the Arabian boundaries by garrisons at Daphe, defending Egypt against the Arabs and the Syrians, and the Libyan border was held from the Greeks by troops stationed at Marea.

The entire portion of the Egyptian population which belonged to neither the priestly cast nor the military cast composed the third order of the State, the common cast. Agriculture, industry and commerce were ascribed to them by general regulations and customs strengthened by time and habit.

The extraordinary fertility of the land and a beneficial climate; excellent laws arrived at through time and experience; an active and benevolent administration, constantly trying to strengthen public order in country as well as city; the inevitable influence of religion on a naturally pious people of

docile character, considered by Herodotus as the most religious of men; all these lead on to believe that the common class in Egypt was happy, and that busy and productive, moderate in its ways as in its wishes, it found in its work the sources of long life and ease.

Families of this cast were usually of considerable size; one finds on the simplest monuments, painted on a wood panel or sculpted in a limestone tile, representing the funeral duties carried out for a father by all of his children, that the number of children of both sexes was eight to twelve and sometimes greater.

The common class usually wore a short, linen tunic called a *calasiris,* tied with a belt just above the hips, sometimes with short sleeves and a bottom hem decorated with fringe. Shoes were made of papyrus or leather, but were probably reserved for the upper classes. The head was normally left uncovered; hair was curly or braided; a woolen coat was sometimes worn over the tunic, removed at the entrance to the temple. In addition to the tunic, women wore full garments of linen or cotton, with wide sleeves, solid colored or striped, in white or solid colors, and their hair was skillfully arranged; their head, hands and ears were decorated with ribbons, buckles and rings. A light shoe covered their feet; they went about with their faces bare, accompanied by several women helpers, of which there were often quite a number in the home. Also dressed in ample garments of striped fabric, these attendants had their hair combed and falling to the shoulders; in addition they wore a large apron made of the same fabric as their dress, neither jewel nor other ornament, and held themselves in respect of the lady of house. Girls taken out from childhood were dressed like their mothers, with the exception of head ornaments; children of both sexes, until eight or nine years of age, wore no more than earrings.

The race was a beautiful one, tall, generally slender, and long-lived, as proven by funerary

Two couples: an official and his wife, on the right (note the tenderness of the wife's gesture), and, on the left, the royal couple of Nefertiti.

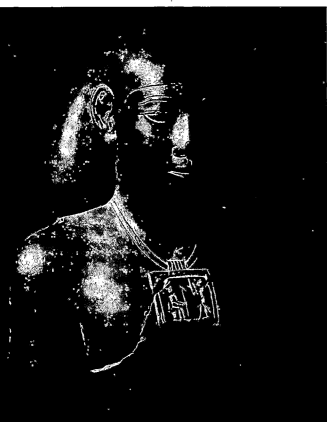

inscriptions, often giving the age of the deceased as over eighty.

Family life was marked by gentle manners and customs of affection. The Paternal authority was all-powerful in Egypt, not by law but by custom; old age was highly respected; when young people met an elderly person, they moved aside to make way for him to pass. Such consideration and feeling were especially carried out in the home.

Homes weve spacious and several stories high. The rooms that made them up had uses analagous to similar ones today. In one avea we see large supplies of various edibles piled on shelves; in another part of the house the floor is covered with a braided, rattan mat in several colors; small latticed windows light the rooms on the ground floor; on the first floor, which was made up of bedrooms, we find, as we do today in all of Egypt's cities, only very small casement windows. The colors of the paintings that provide us with these details indicate that these windows were made of two folding-doors, and were decorated with squares of colored glass. An attic open at both ends and an uncovered terrace completed the building. A garden was attached to the house, and contained a variety of plants; there we fruit trees set in the open air, among which we can distinguish pomegranate and lemon trees; decorative trees in the shape of a pyramid, green groves and vine arbors were both useful and pleasurable. The vines were regularly watered; grapes that had not been eaten in daily consumption were gathered; the cut grapes were then carried in baskets to a vat placed between two palm trees; the grapes were immediately crushed by men holding onto a rope which was strung from one tree to the other. Additional grapes were added to the supply of foods in the house. The religious interdiction of pork was a dietetic and sanitary measure quite wide-spread in the Orient, and it was not only the Egyptian who,

This page: a member of the Amarnian family (Cairo) and a high official. Right: woman with ducks, detail of a fresco.

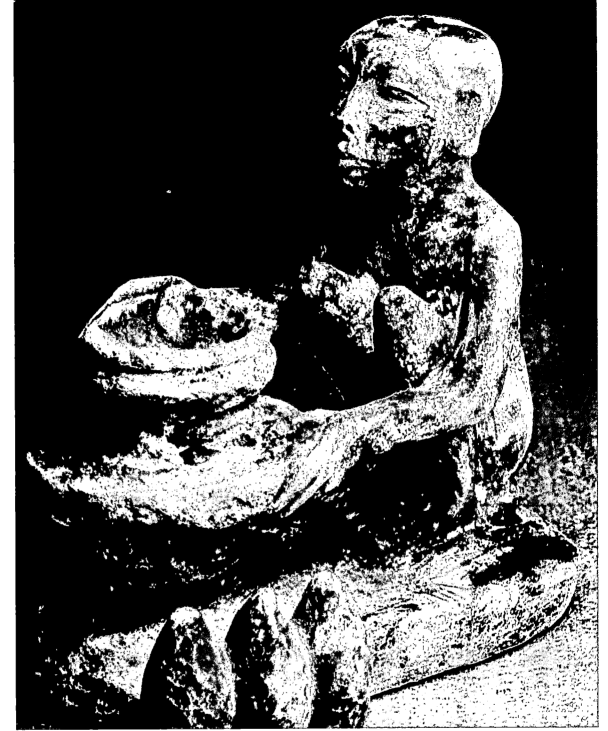

Daily life depicted in art: workers in vineyards or trampling on the grapes; a flock of ducks; the presentation of offerings; craftsmen at work (note the realistic portrayal of the potter's face and body).

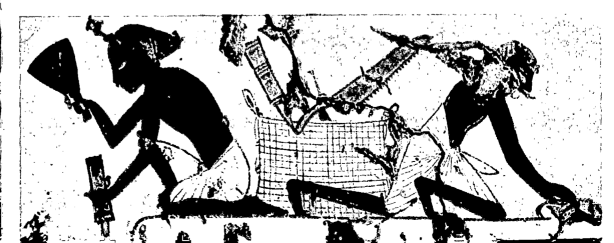

for this reason, refused to kiss any Greek on the mouth, or be served with his knife, skewer or cooking-pot; such principles exist still today.The use of beans was also expressly forbidden; they were not sown, and those plants which happened grow at random were carefully uprooted. This vegetable was considered unclean. Herodotus reports that Egyptians ate ae their meals outside their house; but there is no proof of such a custom in any known monument.

The most common food of the entire population was bread made with wheat flour, called *sorgho* by Herodotus. He adds that breads made from *sorgho* were called *cylletes;* several of these breads have existed until today, collected, like so many other objects, in the tombs; there are different kinds and shapes; there are an equal number of variations seen on monuments. In addition to meat and fish, honey and several kinds of fruit were also part of the Egyptian's basic diet.

Al Herodotus' time, the common drink of the Egyptians was a kind of wine made from barley; the historian adds that there were no vineyards in Egypt. Monuments condradict this statement; not only is the offering of wine to the gods most frequently shown in religious performances, which proves that wine was hardly rare, but one often finds as well, among representations of the fields and harvests, the cultivation of vines, the gathering of the grapes, and the making of wine, which is then placed in large jars which are well stopped, these then stored in cellars.

Nevertheless, the water of the Nile was used by all, and if the ancients deified the river as the creator and source of Egypt, they owed it no less gratitude for the essentially beneficial qualities of its waters. Chemical analysis has provided amazing proof of the extraordinary purity of the Nile's water; this water is as fine for the preparation of food as it is for the arts of chemistry, where it can replace rainwater, non-existent in this country, and distilled water, difficult to obtain in great quantity in a country where fuels are rare. It is especially beneficial and healthful for the human race; it is perhaps the healthiest of all waters on earth; and

Below: a young slave-girl serving her masters or their guests, with a well-stocked buffet; right: procession of bearers of offerings (fresco from funeral chamber).

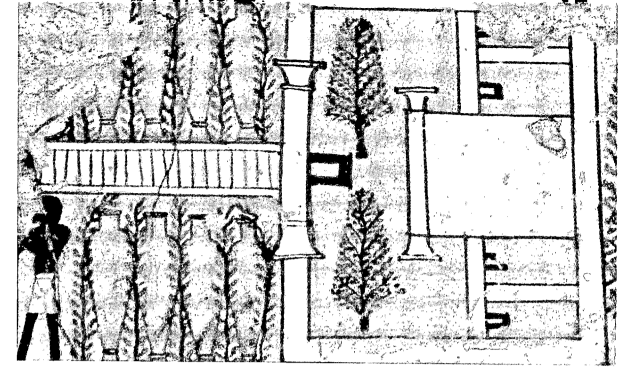

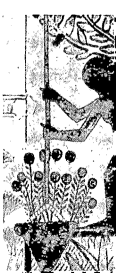

without attributing supernatural virtues with which until very recently tradition had unhesitatingly endowed it, this water is given unanimous praise by those who, either foreigner or native, have used it in all seasons, easily believing that there exists in Constantinople a supply for the Sultan and his family.

The ancient Egypians constantly searched for ways of making this ever so necessary water drinkable at all times, since during three months of the year, the river's flooding made it cloudy, reddish and thick because of its silt content, indeed upleasant, less to the taste than to the eye. They succeeded, discovering that to clarify this water at any time they only needed to rub the rim or the insides of the vessel containing the water with crushed, bitter almonds. This is the same process used by the Egyptians today, successful and proven through thousands of years. Nothing is more common than to see among the representations of the customs of ancient Egypt, in houses, fields, gardens and working places, jars full of water, set on a wooden tripod, in a sheltered corner of a house, in the shade of a tree or in the open air, cooled by servants who fanned the air around them. Moreover, one can not doubt that the ancients anticipated the moderns in indispensable precautions taken for supplying water to cities at some distance from the banks of the Nile, by means of its branches and canals; the flooding

was regulated in such a way that the river, either by its rising or by canals, filled reservoirs meant for this customary supply; and if we recall the peculiar shape of the Nile valley, its surface rather like a donkey's back, with the river at the highest point, we can then see with what ease, almost without any work at all in such a silty terrain, the waters of the Nile could be channeled to the inhabited areas farthest from the borders of the flooding, and how this river, spreading its benefits benefits throughout Egypt, made fruitful its soil, abundantly providing one of man's greatest needs, this river which wholly deserved the altars and worship given to it in gratitude by a renowned and powerful nation.

All its monuments reveal this power in the luxury of its homes and their furnishing.

A spacious garden was usually attached to the Egyptian house. It was square, and enclosed by a wooden fence; one side of the garden faced the Nile, and a row of trees cut in conical forms ran between the Nile and the fence. The entrance was on this side, and a double row of palm trees and pyramid-shaped trees shaded a wide alley which ran along the four sides of the garden. In the center there was a large vine-arbor, while the remainder of the area was covered with squares planted with trees and flowers, and in four symmetrically placed water basins there lived aquatic birds; there was a small day pavilion where one could sit

56

in the shade; lastly, toward the back of the garden, between the vine-arbor and the wide alley, there was another pavilion with several rooms; the first was enclosed and lighted by balconies with low railings; the three others, open to the day, contained fruits, water and other offerings. These pavilions were sometimes constructed as a balustraded

Plan and model of private gardens (11th dynasty). Bottom: gardener drawing water (detail of fresco).

rotunda topped by a depressed vault.

Frescoes decorated the interiors of these houses; their decorative forms were extremely varied; brilliant, beautifully combined colors formed an infinité number of designs, quite suited as well to contempory taste.

Furnishings in ordinary and rare and exotic woods, in metal decorated with sculpted gildings; fabrics in solid colors, embossed, embroidered, dyed, painted, in linen, cotton or silk, locally manufactured or imported; all these contributed to the

pleasure of Egyptian houses and the comforts ot family life. Beds, provided with mattresses, were shaped in the form of a lion, a jackal, a bull or a sphinx, standing on its four legs.

Arm-chairs, trimmed and covered in rich fabrics, were also decorated with different religious or historical sculpture; shepherds supported a chair, symbolizing their servitude. Other arm-chairs were made of cedar wood, inlaid with ivory and ebony, and simple chairs of solidly braided rattan. Small and large round tables, game tables, and boxes of all sizes corresponded in their material and beautiful execution to the splendor of the furnishings. Mats and carpets in bright and varied colors, sometime with historical designs, or the prepared skins of wild animals, covered the floors of the apartments or their most frequented parts; vases, in gold, precious materials, gilded metals, decorated with enamels or fine stones, of an elegance and variety of form that has been preserved for us in the Greek masterpieces, completed the furnishings of an Egyptian house; and following these accounts we can then try to imagine the magnificence of the palaces.

Undoubtedly this luxury and this splendor were unknown to the laborer, artisan and indeed most of the population; but in Egypt, as in other countries, in order to diminish this sharp contrast, considered above all in relation to man's genuine needs, in all that adds to his nourishment and health and supplies his existence with the means of fulfilling his tastes and spirit, and help him recognize and maintain his dignity, we must not forget that the development of luxury in the upper classes does not always indicate misery in the lower classes.

The rearing of animals was one of the great agricultural riches of Egypt; such property was highly regarded in this country, and was surely not mere vain ostentation; but this industry must have been more profitable in lower Egypt, a vast plain which was completely watered by the Nile, than in upper Egypt, a narrow valley where the fertile land could not be used in large part as pasture-ground. It is also in a hypogeum near the pyramids that we find a painting which bears witness to this statement. We see an Egyptian inspecting his herds; he is standing, wearing his *calasyris* tied with a belt; a guardian or shepherd prods the numerous kinds of beasts in the troop; above each herd, the number of heads is clearly marked in numbers which are very much in evidence. The procession is headed by male and female donkeys, lead by a foal;

The riches of the earth (the harvest, Ramosa tomb) and of the water (fishing scene on the abundantly stocked Nile River).

their number is 860;

It has also been noticed in the paintings of another tomb, which seems to have been that of a great Memphis family, that certain servants made offerings of the chief products of their estate to the deceased member of the family, such as dates, figs, pineapples, calves, geese, gazelles, fruits and flowers, among these servants there are several who lead large oxen on leashes, black and red and black and white, wearing collars that end in an ornament in the shape of a lotus flower.

In all such paintings, the master of the house is always recognizable by the long cane he carries in his hand, or upon which he leans to rest.

Other civil scenes painted in tombs lead us to believe that the head of the family was vested with great authority in his house, and had the right of jurisdiction over his servants. We have already mentioned disloyal servants who, at harvest time, crouching on their hands and knees, were taught a lesson and beaten in front of their masters.

It we were to indicate all that the monuments tell us about the work and amusements of the inhabitants of the banks of the northern Nile, there would remain a great deal to add to these details of Egyptian family life, dating back to ten centuries before the poems of Homer. Hunting and fishing were common pleasures for them. Four-legged animals and birds were hunted; greyhounds chased the ostrich or gazelle, the arrow struck the desert beast, nets captured aquatic fowl; paintings of these scenes show us in extraordinarily rich detail the different kinds of animals chased and caught by the hunter,

Scenes showing the raising and slaughtering of livestock.

When the Nile returned to its bed after the perodic flooding, the work of cultivating the land began. "Everyone," says Herodotus, "then sows his his seeds and releases his animals on this land; the seed is thusly well buried in the earth, and the farmer need only await the harvest. The Egyptians, particularly those who live south of Memphis, then reap the most abundant crops with the least work; they do not need to uselessly dig furrows with a plow, nor spade and turn up the earth. They are subject to none of the labors to which other men are condemned in order to reap from the land, since the river spreads over the fields and withdraws when it has watered them." The numerous agricultural scenes in Egyptian works generally confirms Herodotus' reports; we clearly see what was needed for a loose and light soil like the Nile's silt; first a light tilling with a plow to which two oxen or cows were attached by means of a collar and not a yoke, as in other countries. A worker directed the oxen with a stick, while

Scenes of merriment: the Egyptians liked their festivities to be accompanied by music and entertainment.

The flute, the lute and the harp were the most commonly used instruments.

The harp was given preference over the lute and the flute (details from funerary frescoes).

The guests were seated according to very strict etiquette.

Slaves adorning their mistresses before a reception or dancing for them, like these dancer-acrobats (top left) on a low-relief from an 18th-dynasty tomb.

Above: the table used in the 'snake game' (not unlike our 'snakes and ladders'). Below: four girls playing ball. Right-hand page: a curious instrument used in playing the game 'of the dog and the jackal'.

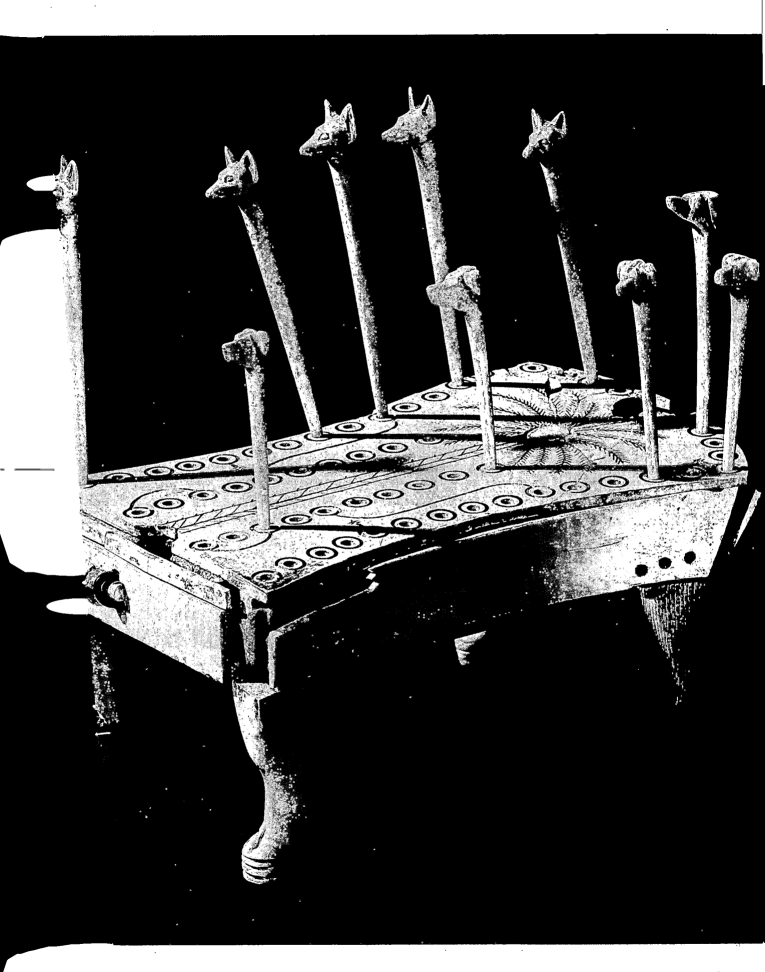

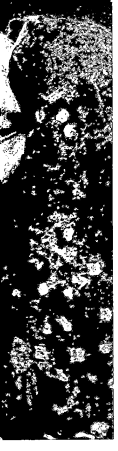

another held the arm of the plough. Sometimes three or four men were used for the job, easily pulling a rope attached to the plough. This instrument was usually made of hard wood, the ground only rarely requiring a metal ploughshare. The same was true for the hoe and the spade, used by hand in the less demanding jobs of the fields. The seeds were then thrown to the ground thusly prepared, and then rather than covering the sown seeds by another tillage, the herds of animals were released on the land in order to trample and thus bury the seeds.

Horses, donkeys and oxen were also used for agricultural labors; and it is to be supposed that in sowing for a second harvest

Pectoral, finery decorating the bust of a queen, and woman's wig sprinkled with gold. Above: low-relief on a tomb.

in the same year, on the same land, which was necessarily more resistant than immediately after the flooding, one used for this tillage a wooden ploughshare trimmed with metal: it is believed that they were constructed in this way, judging from the monuments. Two-wheeled chariots, pulled by oxen or horses, were also used in working the land, suitably constructed for the country's soil.

A few months after the sowing came that of the wheat harvests; reapers cut handfuls just below the spikes; behind them came women and children who gathered the spikes in sacks; jars of water, for refreshment and slaking thirst, stood on tripods near the reapers; these vases, made of porous clay, are still used in Egypt. One of these vessels known as a *gouleh,* or *bardague,* is the best known; it is light, portable, and of an elegant shape, most useful and found everywhere.

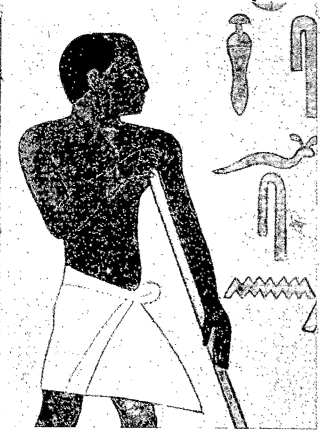

To the number of natural products commonly used for nourishment, we must add those mentioned by Herodotus as peculiar to the inhabitants of Egypt's marshy areas. To obtain their food, he says they resorted to several means: when the river was swollen and covered the neighboring countryside, it carried with its waters a great quantity of a kind of lily called a lotus by the Egyptian (the *nymphoea lotus* of modern botany). They gathered these plants and dried them in the sun; from these they extracted a seed which was made into a dough which they baked as bread. The lotus root was also edible, being quite sweet to the taste; another variety of lily produced seeds the size of an olive pit, good to eat raw or dried; the stem of the papyrus was also a common food: to make it more tender it was baked in an oven; lastly, fish, cleaned and simply dried in the sun, was the most

common food of the inhabitants of Egypt's most wet regions.

Vegetables were particularly a part of the diet of children, generally quite numerous in each family, by dint of the law which, not distinguishing between legal and illegal wives, considered all children of the same

A rather large variety of fruits was also part of the diet; the fig and other similar trees flourished on Egyptian soil; marshy terrain also contributed melons and watermelons. Garlic and the onion were quite famous, at least to the point of being mentioned in history for their agreeable flavors.

Details of funerary frescoes portraying work in the fields, from plowing to harvest.

Lotus flowers, shown above in their natural state, are a constant decorative theme on the steles, murals and temple columns of ancient Egypt. Here, the temple of Amon, at Karnak.

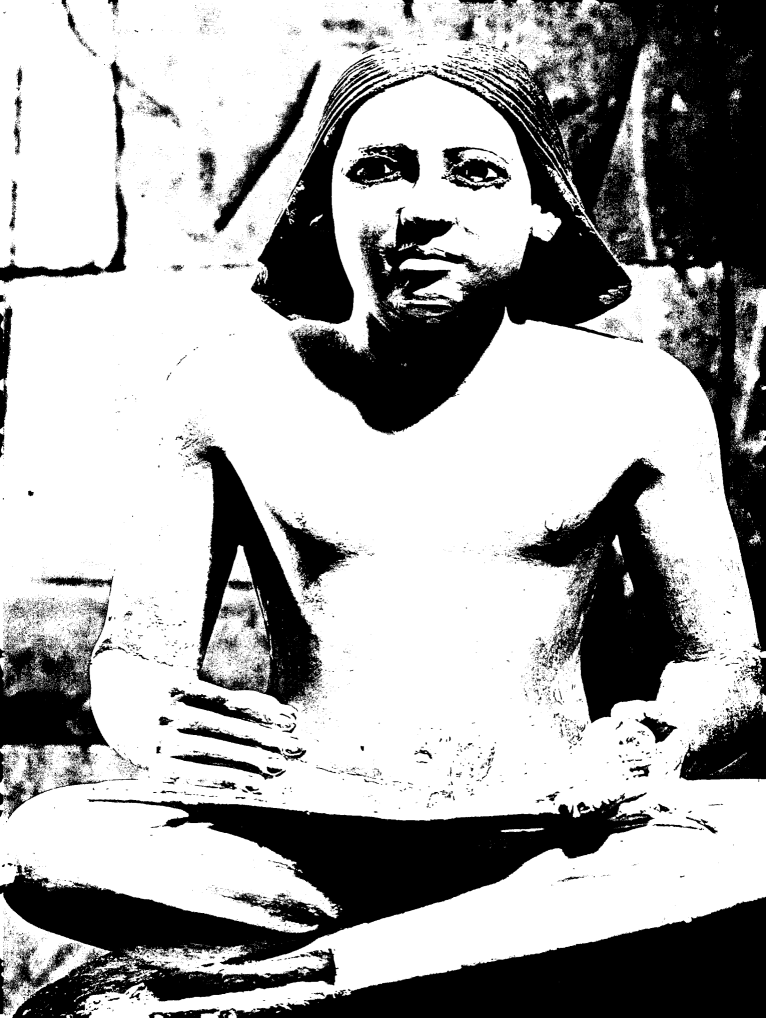

8 - From goldwork to writing

Egypt had constructed great architectural monuments several centuries before the coming of Abraham. Barbarians destroyed them; and in the 20th century B.C., freed from these military murderers of arts and laws, it rebuilt temples to its gods; debris from the ancient edifices was used, and we still find today in monuments such debris that dates back thirty-seven centuries. Sculpture and painting decorated these edifices, and furnishings and clothing was in keeping with their magnificence. Stones and precious metals, rich fabrics, increased in valve by their extraordinary labor, these were used in the pomp of ceremonies, carried out with art and taste. Very early travelers in Egypt used the metals they found in this country. Abraham gave Rebecca a ring and bracelets of gold; Joseph received a ring and a necklace of gold from a Pharaoh, and had his silver cup put in his brother Benjamin's sack of wheat. Fabrics dyed purple, scarlet and crimson, wool, goat or camel hair, linen,

Two very different occupations: that of the scribe (the eyes of this extremely lifelike statue are inlaid with crystal, alabaster and bronze), and that of the hunter (ivory-plated panel from chest; Cairo).

byssus, coloring and aromatic substances, all these are mentioned in writings of the same period. Egypt knew as well how to create less refined products which were nonetheless equally useful to the public and domestic economies; lampblack and ivoryblack were made, and a strong glue from the hide of cattle; live sheep were dyed purple, and wool was whitened with sulphurous steam; it was known that if a lighted lamp plunged into a vat or an underground place goes out, it is unsafe.

The art of enameling was certainly practiced by inhabitants of Thebes. We find the products of this art everywhere, as well as white and colored porcelaine of the greatest perfection; in addition to the finesse of the workmanship there was the elegance of form. Cobalt blue is a most commonly used color in Egyptian sculpture, and modern chemistry has confirmed that cobalt and other colors of a metallic base, used to cover Egyptian statues had a powerful biting effect and penetrated sandstone and granite to an amazing degree.

It is therefore quite certain that the art of making and treating glass and enamel was highly perfected in Egypt. Glass was also worked with wire and welded with sulphur; glass and enamel were used to decorate temples and palaces, which were paved with

gleaming, brilliant tiles.

Homer enumerates the gifts that Helen and Menelaus received from the king and queen of Egypt: there was a basket, two bowls and two tripods in silver, a gold frog, and another silver basket with gold handles.

If we consider the material processes of Egyptian architecture, we will find several rules quite different from those used in Europe, since it had other available means. Egyptian architecture was born in Egypt, the first fact demonstrated by its study. Each people imitated the form of nature he found around him: the Egyptians made their capitals of palm leaves, and the Greeks used acanthus leaves; Europe imitated Greece and never equaled its perfection. In Greek architecture as in modern architecture, the architrave is placed directly on the capital; in Egyptian architecture on the contrary, a square block, placed on the capital, supports the architrave, because the Egyptians had felt that this part of the entablature which always has such a heavy appearance, could not be properly placed on capitals composed of leaves, flowers and delicate ornaments. The result of this uniquely Egyptian principle was that the capitals were separated from the architrave, the main lines, which are always a source of beauty in architecture, were not broken, and were as such the outstanding characteristic of Egyptian architecture.

Egyptian nautical construction does not seem to have been perfected, as seen in bas-reliefs showing battles at sea; but if accounts of history are not doubted, then the Egyptians were true navigators, crossing the Red Sea, having dealings with the peoples of the coasts of southern African and eastern India; and that Sesotris had a fleet of four hundred sailing ships built with which he conquered all the maritime provinces and all the islands of the Eritrean sea, as far as India.

The Egyptian colonies arriving in Greece before and after the time of Sesostris could only have been carried there by large, safe ships.

Thebes, the religious and political capital of Egypt, was also its richest and most visited commercial city; it was centrally located between the Mediterranean, the Red Sea and Ethiopia, and in this position was the natural market for the ships and products of these different countries. It is in this royal city, the center of eastern commerce, that all kinds of riches, says Homer, were accumu-

lated, and by the arriving caravans, was in contact with neighboring countries of the Niger and Carthage.

The origin of the Egyptian language is inknown; we find it in the oldest monuments of Egypt and Nubia, and if it was descended, along with the population, from the upper regions of the Nile, it would then be in these ancient regions that we would have to search for its birth.

Inscriptions from all periods of the Egyptian monarchy, pharaonic, Ethiopian, Persian, Greek or Roman, prove without a doubt the constant usage of the same national idiom in Egypt. In quantities of private, civil contracts, or in writings on various subjects, some dating earlier than the time of Moses, others contemporary with the Roman emperors, the same idiom is used. Before the courts of justice in the time of the Greek domination, only a contract written in the Egyptian language was authorized by law, and the execution of this contract translated into Greek was not sufficient to sustain a right. Even in Roman times, holy prayers

Left: on a wooden tablet covered with stucco, a sketch with grid pattern, used to establish the proportions of the human body (British Museum). Above, the restoration of ancient works.

enclosed in mummies' coffins were written in the Egyptian language; and all these facts are shown by papyrus manuscripts preserved in our museums.

Ancient Egyptian writing is generally known as *hieroglyphic writing,* composed of *signs* called *hieroglyphs,* and which are in effect as the etymology indicates, *sacred, sculpted characters.* These signs do not have a uniform expression, and the differences, which divide them into three classes, probably indicate the origin and successive perfecting of the graphic system as it is known today.

This system of writing was adequate for the uses of the people who, having imagined it, completely possessed its theory and practice, but only so far as there was no need to communicate their intelligible writing to foreign societies or individuals. But as soon as this need manifested itself, and one had to write the name of a single foreigner, figurative, symbolic or tropical signs were no longer adequate, because the foreigner's name, having no sense in the language of the people who wanted to write it, and thusly giving no *idea,* could not be written by signs that expressed only ideas.

Thus one arrived, how it is not known, at the sounds which formed this name, and one

understood at the same time what use these signs which expressed these sounds would be: the newest and last progesss in the graphic art, which was the most ingeniously perfected, and very well adapted to the languages of the time, which were for the most part formed of words and roots of one syllable. One therefore introduced the use of sound signs, generally called *phonetic,* and whose choice was not difficult, for one only had to choose among the figurative signs, for each syllable to express phonetically the sign representing an object whose name in the spoken language was this same syllable: thus the disk of the sun expressed the syllable *re,* because this syllable was the name of the sun, and so on. The Chinese arrived at this syllabic system, and preserved it, unchanged to today, for writing foreign names and words in their language. In the same manner, the Egyptians arrived at a truly *alphabetic* system, and introduced this into their system of writing without changing the nature of their drawn signs.

As for the expression or graphic value of the signs, the theory is as uncertain as their material classification.

Figurative signs quite simply expressed the idea of the object whose forms they reproduced; the idea of a horse, a lion, an obelisk, a stele, a crown, a chapel, etc., is expressed graphically by the shape of each of these objects; the meaning of the characters is certain in each case.

The *symbolics,* or tropicals or enigmatics, expressed a metaphysical idea by an image of a physical object whose qualities had an analogy, according to the Egyptians, direct or indirect, evident or far-removed, with the idea to be expressed. Each kind of character seems to have been searched out and invented for abstrait ideas, dealing with religion, or royal power, so intimately linked with the religious system. The bee was the symbolic sign for the idea of king; raised arms were the idea of offering and offerings; a vase whose water was spilling out was the idea of libation, etc.

Phonetic signs expressed the sounds of the spoken language, and had, in Egyptian writing, the same functions as the letters of the alphabet in ours.

Hieroglyphic writing is thusly essentially different from the writing generally used today in the main point that it used at the

Above: scribe portrayed on the low-relief of a tomb. Right: the famous Denderah Zodiac, now in the Louvre.

78

same time, in the same text, in the same sentence and sometimes in the same word, three kinds of characters, *figurative, symbolic* and *phonetic,* while our modern writing, in this way similar to the writings of other peoples in classic antiquity, uses only *phonetic* characters, that is, alphabetic. to the exclusion of all others.

This however, did not result in confusion, since the science of this writing was generally established in the country.

What we have learned from the monuments on the subject of the ancient Egyptians' numeric system, proves that their arithmetic was no more perfected than that of the Greeks; they were unaware of the important function of zero, and the valve of position in number signs; ingenious, fruitful processes by means of which, with nine numbers of increasing valve, each time multiplied by ten, as we move to the left, we can, in the modern system of the Indians via the Arabs, conveniently express the highest numbers.

No written theories have survived on the Egyptians' arithmetic; once the number signs were recognized, all such written signs on monuments were collected, and necessarily incomplete conclusions were drawn, in the sense that one must not think that the Egyptians were unaware of a certain part of the science of numbers because the theory is not found in the monuments. We know how important the knowledge of geometry was in their civilization; we can see in the precision of their monuments and their magnificent architectural creations to what extent they called upon this science; thusly we cannot conclude that they did not have theories whose application we find in such great number.

We must realize that the sages of Egypt had precise ideas on the length of the solar year, but nevertheless did not introduce them into the civil calendar to be used in the Egyptian empire; this knowingly irregular calendar, counted only 365 complete days.

It was this calendar which was used in Egypt as far back as the annals of time go, despite the changes which at different times upset the nationally established order and customs of Egypt. The use of this calendar was one of the numerous public institutions that political Alexandria ordered to be respected; the Romans modified it, but at the same time adopted it concerning all the acts of its administration which especially applied to Egypt.

Hieroglyphic script used figurative, symbolic and phonetic characters. Right: portrayal of the god Ihy (Cairo Museum, Treasure of Tutankhamun).

9 - Deification. The cult of the dead

According to several Greek and Roman authors, the worship of certain animals and products of the earth was one of the rules of the Egyptian religion. The first Greek travelers, witnesses of certain religious ceremonies, did not understand the symbolic expression, and saw only the material aspect. Following a connection between several of these ceremonies and celestial phenomena, they assumed that the religion was based entirely on astronomy, and tried to interpret in this way all the sacred myths, even those whose sources and true motives were most evidently quite different.

It is according to such witnesses as these that the ancient Egyptian philosophers, teachers of one of the most illustrious nations that ever existed, were declared to be ignorant of the concept of a god, deep in the shadows of polytheism, worshiping only material goods, or simply, blind, blasphemous and atheistic.

Several more clear-sighted philosophers,

Left: imperial tomb at Thebes. Above: funerary inscription.

however, more impartial and capable of serious study, little by little neared the truth, and were compensated for the difficulties of their observations. Propnyry dared to affirm that the Egyptians formerly knew only one god; Herodotus had also said that the Thebans had the idea of a single god who had had no beginning and was immortal.

A few words suffice to sum up the true and complete idea of Egyptian religion: it was a pure *monotheism,* manifesting itself externally by a *symbolic polytheism,* that is to say, a single god whose qualities and attributes were personified in an equal number of active agents or obedient divinities.

We cannot omit, in the discussion of Egyptian religion, the reminder that in Egypt more than in any modern society, faith and worship were combined with man's intimate life. Religion controlled his actions with absolute authority; it became his master at birth, not even abandoning him after his death. It promised him honorable funeral ceremonies according to his rank, and a resting place where his remains would always be sheltered from insult, either in a family tomb or in a public tomb. Finally, religion prescribed for all the use of certain practices, ingeniously discovered, for the almost eternal preservation of the human body, the last considerate homage to the dignity of the race.

We are indebted to this Egyptian custom for the innumerable quantity of embalmed human bodies which have come down to us perfectly preserved and which we call mummies. We will summarize the aspects of this quite popular subject which will most interest the reader.

Herodotus speaks in precise terms of the customs of Egypt concerning funeral ceremonies and mourning. When the head of the family died, all women members covered their foreheads with mud and went about dishevelled in the city. The men followed the same custom for women.

After these first expressions of suffering, the body of the dead was immediately taken to the embalmer, a lower class of the priesthood. The family settled upon a price for his services, depending upon the simplicity or magnificence of the embalming. There were in effect, several classes. The most common was restricted to purging one's insides with the cheapest of drugs, drying out the entire body, leaving it in native sodium carbonate for seventy days, then shrouding it in a winding-sheet of coarse linen, even more roughly sewn up, and thusly placed in the public catacombs. The body was at times stretched out on a plank of sycambre wood which was also wrapped in the same, coarse linen.

If a limited expense was possible, cedar oil was used to cleanse the insides; the body was dried in the same natron formula; the limbs, separately, or the entire body, were wrapped in little bands of cotton soaked in the same oil, or in another preserving substance; the body was then enclosed in a coffin more or less decorated with paintings. The name of the dead, that of his mother, and his profession, were usually written on the coffin, which was made of wood.

The embalmer's first operation was to remove the brain via the nostrils by means of a curved instrument; the cavity of the head was then filled with an injection of a pure, bituminous liquid, which hardened as it cooled. The brain's lining, perfectly preserved, has been removed from several mummies' heads.

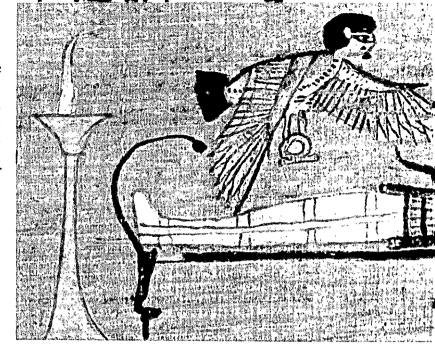

The eyes were also removed and were replaced with enamel eyes.

The hair was not removed, and has been found at times long, braided, matted, and arranged in such a way that revealed the hairdresser's hand.

With a sharp stone, an incision was made in the left side; through this opening the intestines and vital organs were removed. The cavities of the abdomen and the chest were carefully washed with decoctions of palm wine or aromatics and wiped with powdered aromatics; they were then filled with myrrh and other perfumes, even the sawdust of fragrant woods, mixed with jewels and religious figurines in precious or common metals, hard stones or porcelaine.

The interior of the corpse thusly prepared,

it was then placed in the natron, a most common substance in Egypt throughout the ages, and left in it for seventy days; the flesh and the muscles were completely eaten away, all that remained of the body being the skin clinging to the bones. Such is the state of several mummies that have been found and examined.

Often, rather than drying out the body in this way, there was injected in all the veins, by complicated and costly processes, a chemically composed liquid with the property of preserving the body while leaving it all its natural elasticity.

At the same time, the intestines and the principle vital organs were placed in a preparation of boiling bitumen; the brain, the heart and the liver were separately wrapped in linen, and all were placed in four vases, filled with the liquid in which they had been boiled. These four vases are commonly called the *canopic vases*. They were made from all kinds of matters, from baked clay to striped, oriental alabaster and granite.

After the seventy days of immersion in the natron, the body was shrouded. Each finger was separately wrapped in narrow strips; the hand was then done, and the arm separately. The same operation was carried out on the other limbs, and the head was even more delicately cared for. The finest linen, or sometimes a very beautiful muslin was in direct contact with the skin. Several layers covered the face, and adhesion is such that when removed as a whole, these layers have been able to serve as a mold for making a plaster portrait of the deceased.

The entire length of the body was then wrapped, and the original shapes of the limbs were skillfully recreated with the strips of linen, having been completely eaten away by the natron.

It has been noticed in this class mummy, that the nails of the hands and feet were gilded; gold forms have been found on the eyes and mouth, and the head entirely gilded as well; lastly, the bodies of royalty were

Death and the beliefs which surrounded it, as shown in the famous Papyrus of Ani (or Book of the Dead), from the 17th century B.C.

completely covered in fold, or even wrapped in a first layer of gold, a kind of embossed casing which reproduced in relief their portrait and all the forms of the body.

Before using the strips which completely covered the body, the arm was placed in a position regulated by custom and law: women's hands were crossed on the stomach; men's arms remained by their sides; sometimes the left hand was placed on the right shoulder, thusly forming a sling on the chest.

On these same bodies have been found, either under all the winding cloths or among the layers, rings on the fingers of the mummies and necklaces on their throats, various jewels, figurines, sentimental objects, miniature pieces of furniture and pieces of different fabrics; lastly there were manuscripts placed at the sides of the body or between the legs, and wrapped, like the body, in bitumen and strips of cloth.

It would also seem, according to the state of several mummies, that after these preparations, they were plunged fully dressed into a vat of boiling bitumen, which penetrated as far as the bones' marrow, and once cooled, were no more than a mass of unchangeable, hardened bitumen.

Thus wrapped in strips and a shroud held by crossed ribbons of fabric, the mummy, with no visible trace of a corpse or of these preparations, was placed in a coffin of wood, granite, basalt or other matter. The coffin was decorated with painting and sculpture; for persons of high rank, the first coffin was placed in a second, and the second in a third, all equally decorated in religious subjects, the orthodox repetition of the scenes of the great funeral ritual, in which we see the soul of the deceased visiting and making offerings to all the gods whose protection it solicited.

It is also in these coffins that manuscripts have been found, portions, more or less complete, of the great funerary manuscript, this *book of manifestation to the light,* a considerable number of copies of which are found in European museums, because this book of prayers was part of the Egyptian's funeral furnishings.

Human mummies are to be found in all museums; those of men are recognized by

the appendage of a braided beard, attached to the chin, not found on those of women. Mummies of children are rare, while those of different animals are very common. One must not forget that these animals symbolized certain gods, and that these animals were fed while they were alive, and embalmed only after death. The ibis was dedicated to Thoth, and one finds at Hermopolis (the city of Hermes or Thoth) thousands of ibis mummies, as elsewhere one finds mummies of cats, crocodiles, mongeese, sparrow-hawks, fish, snakes, cattle and rams; unquestionable witnesses in behalf of the highest expression manifested for the symbolism of these creatures, as opposed to the idea of direct worship, in the religious precepts of Egypt.

Decoration of the chapel of Anubis in the Thebes necropolis. Right: a mummy being presented to the dead man's wife. Left: Anubis and Thoth weighing the heart of a dead man in the presence of the god Horus (painting from a casket; Louvre).

10 - The Pyramids

It was the Kings of the third dynasty who had built the pyramids of Sakkarah and Dashur; these are the oldest known monuments of man's hand in the world.

The fourth dynasty was remarkable in the number of princes who made it up and the length of their reigns. Its origins located in Memphis, it supplied seventeen kings who occupied the throne for 448 years.

The first on this list was named Souphi. He is spoken of in Egyptian annals as an impious and proud prince; nevertheless, sensing his duties, he wrote a book on holy matters which was held in great esteem by the Egyptians. After a reign of 63 years, his first successor was Sensaouphi, who reigned for 66 years, and after him, Mancheres, whose reign was also 63 years long. In this dynasty were also Soris, Ratoeses, Bicheres, Sebercheres, and Tamphtis.

The pyramids at Gizeh were built by the first three Kings of this dynasty, and served as their tombs. Around these immense monu-

The Pyramids. Left: at Giza, view of the rows of masonry. Above: the mastaba, or step-pyramid, of King Djeser, at Sakkarah: the first royal tomb built in the shape of a pyramid.

ments are found pyramids of lesser dimensions, and tombs constructed of large blocks of stone, burial places for the princes of the families of these ancient kings.

There is only a small distance between the pyramids at Sakkarah in the north, and Gizeh further south, which is covered by desert.

At Sakkarah we find the ancient cemetery of Memphis, called the Plain of Mummies, scattered with pyramids and tombs.

At Gizeh are the most universally famous pyramids; these wonders must be closely studied to be truly appreciated; they seem to gradually diminish in height as one approaches them, and it is only in touching the stone blocks of which they are built, that we get a fair idea of their immensity.

The stone foundation of the great pyramid rests on the very rock of the plain, and this layer is perfectly set in a straight, vertical hollow. Above this first imbedded layer, the rock is cut in regular socle form. The rock of which this pedestal is made, rises approximately one hundred feet above the highest waters of the Nile, forming a solid whose base is not reached even at a depth of two hundred feet. The earth's surface here is a desert, void of all vegetation: man's only evidence are his remains unmercifully exhumed from these tombs.

The materials for this colossal construction were taken from the quarries of Thorrah, on the Nile's right bank, directly opposite Memphis. These quarries of white limestone were mined in the times of the Pharoahs, the Persians, the Ptolemies, the Romans and the Arabs.

The use of these materials is remarkable in that we easily recognize that it would be difficult to match with greater exactitude, to draw straighter lines, and create more perfect joints than the blocks here in the interior construction of the great pyramid. Each sharp-edged block sets into the next; the one below, with a hollow two inches deep, grasps an equal projection of the block above, and each surface is thus held along its entire height; not the slightest fault nor the least deviation can be observed.

The great pyramid is precisely placed so that each of its corners face one of the cardinal points; even today, it is only with the greatest difficulty that that we would succesfully draw such a vast and exact meridian line; and from the location of the great pyramid we have drawn this vitally important fact in the physical history of the globe: it is that in several thousand years the position of the earth's axis has not perceptibly changed; and the great pyramid is the only monument on earth which, by its antiquity, can provide the means for such an observation.

The north-east face of the great pyramid block near the bended junction, precisely closes the two canals off from each other, and in order to bypass this obstacle, one chipped away the softest rocks which formed the right wall of the canal, parallel to the side of the block. Thus one enters the second canal, at the end of which one finds oneself on a landing, and on the right, the opening of a deep well carved in the rock. A horizontal canal also begins there, one hundred and seventeen feet in length. It leads to a chamber called the Queen's Chamber, which is seventeen feet ten inches long, and sixteen feet one inch wide. It is empty.

Returning to the entrance of the horizontal canal, one ascends a new gallery, one hundred twenty-five feet long, twenty-five feet high, and six and a half feet wide. On each side there are benches, twenty-one inches long and nineteen inches wide. Twenty-eight holes, twelve inches wide and six and a half inches deep have been made in each bench. Eight layers of stone, projecting one over the other, form the walls of this gallery and give its ceiling the effect of a vault. At its end one comes to a landing, giving on to a vestibule which leads to an opening which is three feet three inches wide, and three feet five inches high, and seven feet ten inches long; it is the entrance to the upper chamber called the King's Chamber, an entrance originally closed and hidden by blocks of stone.

This chamber is entirely constructed of large granite blocks, perfectly erect and polished.

At the west end of the chamber one sees the sarcophagus, also in granite, seven feet one inch long, three feet one inch wide, and three feet six inches high; it is placed in a north-south position; its cover is not there. There is an empty space above this burial chamber: it is only three feet high; the stones which form this enclosure, also in granite, are erect but not polished, and those of the floor above, that is, the other side of the ceiling of the royal chamber, are uncut and of unegual heights; this void thus creates a double ceiling for the royal chamber, in this way protecting it from the additional weight above.

The well, already indicated at the entrance to the horizontal gallery, is for the most part dug into the rock, in such narrow dimensions (twenty-two inches by twenty-four inches), that a man can barely crouch down but not stand bent over; it is, nevertheless, the work of a man's hand, and is measured at approximately two hundred feet long. Notches cut into its walls make the descent less painful and dangerous. The end of it has not been reached, but in the explored part, one descends to fifty feet below the level of the Nile.

It is in the part of the Libyan chain stretching to the east toward the plain that we find the figure of the sphinx; it is in one of

The Great Pyramid of Giza. Following pages: views of the ruins of Luxor and their famous Colossi.

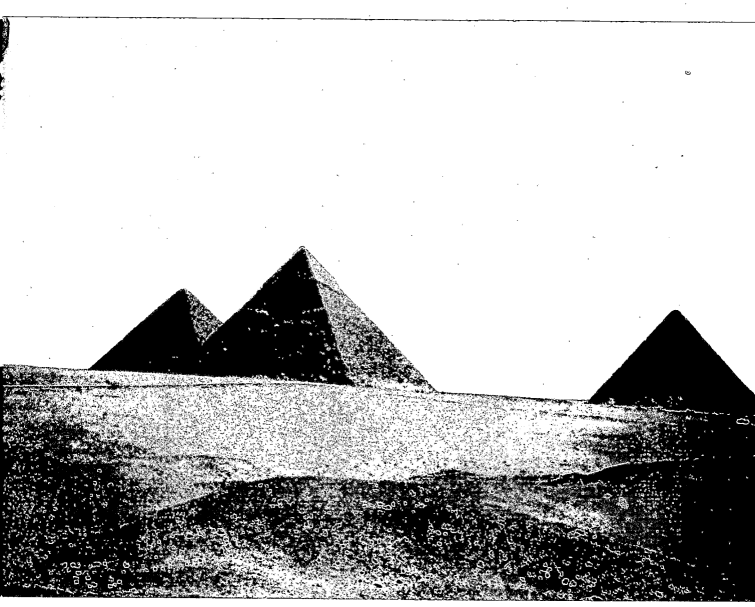

the sides of a break in the chain that it is cut; it is one with the ground ; its height of forty feet above the ground is the witness and measure of the quantity of stone removed from the surface to leave this elevation on the plain. The total length of the monolithic sphinx is one hundred seventeen feet; the contour of the head at the forehead is eighty-one feet; the height from the stomach to the top of the head is fifty-one feet. There is a hole dug several feet deep into the head; it was used to hold the ornaments and the royal or religious coiffure which determined the symbolic expression of the sphinx.

Perhaps the exactitude of this description will serve as an excuse for its monotony. These unchangeable monuments in question were destined from the beginning to strike all successive generations of men with an equally unchangeable admiration, offering itself to them wrapped in enigma, grandeur and memories. Now may the genius of man religiously maintain the preservation of these extraordinary works: they are witnesses to his existence, created before all historic tradition, and are as well the surest and oldest of standards capable of reminding the genealogist of the works of human intelligence.

Giza: the Pyramids seen from the desert, and the Sphinx (whose face was apparently modeled on that of the Pharaoh Kephren, who built the second Great Pyramid). Last page: mortuary barge engraved on the sarcophagus of Ramses III (Louvre).